SHOULD I MARRY?

The Essential Guide to Discernment

Should I Marry?

The Essential Guide to Discernment

Vicente "Tex" S. Hernandez

Polaris Publishing

Manila, 2026

© 2026 Vicente Javier Stabile Hernandez

All rights reserved.

First Edition published in August 2024

Second Edition

No part of this publication may be reproduced, duplicated, or transmitted in any form—electronic or printed—without prior written permission from the author. Recording of this work is strictly prohibited.

Image Credits

Unless otherwise indicated, the images in this book were created using AI-assisted rendering tools, guided by the author's conceptual and compositional direction. These visuals serve as symbolic companions to the text, reflecting its philosophical and emotional themes.

This title—alongside blog articles on related topics and upcoming additions to the series—can be found at echoepolaris.com, echoesofpolaris.com, or by searching on Google Play Books or Amazon Kindle.

Distributed by Amazon Kindle.

> Your love is king, [I] crown you in my heart
> Your love is king, never need to part
> Your love is king, you're the ruler of my heart
>
> Sade, *Your Love is King*

Contents

Introduction 1
Chapter One: 'I Like You' 3
    A Reflection of Oneself 5
    Compatibility 8
    Masculinity and Femininity 9
    Unisex 12
Chapter Two: Harnessing Fear 15
    Technology 17
    Premarital Sex 19
    Permanency and Exclusivity 22
    Maturity 24
Chapter Three: Is It Love? 27
    Forever Love 28
    Loneliness 31
    Manipulation 34
    Genuine Love 35
    The Love-Hurt Dichotomy 37
Chapter Four: The Family Project 39
    Legacy 44

Investing in Your Future 46
Natural Family Planning 47
Chapter Five: I Got Some Questions 51
Values 51
Feelings 54
Children 55
Professional Plans 56
Religious Affiliation 57
Relatives 58
"Am I too old to get married?" 61
Hurt 63
Conclusion 65
Acknowledgments 67
About the Author 69
Other Works by the Author 71
NOTES 73

Introduction

He never made it to church, not that day, not ever. His fiancée was standing and waiting for him in a stunning ball gown. His mother—his father had died years before—and the parents of the bride, together with relatives, groomsmen, and bridesmaids, were there too, waiting, but he had vanished.

He, aided by the two families, had invested in the ceremony, the reception, and the hotel where they were going to spend the wedding night; there were no plans for a honeymoon yet, and they were going to stay, in the meantime, with his mother.

The night before the wedding, he received an unexpected visitor. One of his drinking buddies came over to talk some sense into him: "Lance—not his real name—what are you doing? You're young, smart, and wealthy... Are you awake? Are you going to throw away all your potential for this girl?" Lance was impulsive and had been drinking. It did not take long for him to turn around his future.

With just what he was wearing, he bought a plane ticket to the big city, leaving her behind, with no other intention than looking forward to a happy life of debauchery, something that he would never enjoy. He needed to put some distance and did not set foot in his hometown for at least ten years. He never lived there again, only visiting briefly to see his distressed mother who had taken the weight of the disappointing wedding on her shoulders.

Was it worth it? None would agree with it, but perhaps it was rather beneficial for the bride. A person like Lance who decided to turn around his future so easily was not truly prepared to marry.

There are some telltale signs that, like hand and arm signals, are universal means of nonverbal communication conveying a wide range of messages. What are these messages? What do you have to consider before making a commitment? What do you have to know and learn?

This book is not a rational—or irrational—attempt to discourage anyone but the opposite. We need to put things straight. We also need to consider the fact that, aside from marriage, there is a variety of life commitments that need to be taken seriously.

We will be talking about all this in the next few pages. Like in the case of my first book in the 'Big-Question Series'—'Am I an Atheist?'—I intend to list down questions to facilitate and summarize the discussion.

Chapter One: 'I Like You'

You can gauge the type of party you've crashed by observing the prevailing atmosphere. The vibe at the party gives away its style. Whether it's a 'costume bash,' a 'formal gala,' a 'chic cocktail gathering,' or even a 'relaxed poolside event,' you can tell just by looking. But when you get into a family reunion, the feeling is different; the environment strikes you as heartwarming, lively, and welcoming. Within the family, the guests engage easily in conversation in a cheerful, outgoing atmosphere, which contrasts sharply with the icy formality of professional gatherings we might be accustomed to attending or the wild parties we hear about, which often leave only regrets behind.

Even if you are not on good terms with other family members, you share many things in common with all siblings and closest relatives by natural, family ties. Friends are in a similar category; we grew up with them or met them along the way and they are always welcome. But in professional meetings, notable differences exist in the way people deal with each other, because the meetings' main goal is to foster mutually beneficial relationships.

The nature of our connections to the people we interact with shapes the range of emotions we experience toward them. Additionally, the type of mix that we share—because we feel good around them—brings us closer and closer to one another.

Fig. 1. You can gauge the type of party you've crashed by observing the prevailing atmosphere.

What people relish is important to feel good and make them happy, and what we appreciate in others significantly impacts our feeling of closeness. The more striking your fondness about a person, the more special you feel about him or her, and the memory of any given encounter uplifts you beyond expectations. Have you wondered what compels you to band with that person you met and liked, the one who might one day become your sweetheart? Can you put a name to it? This is a mystery that the psychiatrists, the endocrinologists, and the neurologists are still trying to figure out.

Many call it 'romantic attraction,' the urge to connect with someone and eventually, fall in love with him or her. Attraction boosts our ability to relate and changes the disposition of the person, empowering the senses. What is critical in the way of attraction? Is beauty a key factor?

'According to a 2020 Gallup Korea survey targeting 1,500 men and women aged 19 and above, 89 percent of respondents believed that appearance has a very or somewhat important impact on life. This result is not very different from 1994's 87 percent.'[1]

We would probably agree with the results of the Korean survey too. Appearance might have a lot to do with attraction, but it need not be associated with beauty—you will probably know of many cases where one or the other is not necessarily beautiful. What makes a person lovable? What makes you lovable?

A Reflection of Oneself

The starting point of attraction is likeness; 'I like you.' And for likeness to turn into enduring affection—the preamble of love—we need to consider two factors: first, what you see in the other person which is like a reflection of oneself—the values that you both share, and second, what you find in the other that complements yourself and makes you whole.

At this stage, true love has yet to develop; it hasn't transformed into a mutual longing, which is essential. This will happen later. For now, we need to understand which values and complementarities will function as the catalyst for everything that follows.

Fig. 2. Sharing values is like looking at oneself in a mirror.

Sharing values is like looking at oneself in a mirror. Some couples might even look alike; others seem to resemble each other increasingly over the years. Unconsciously, specific factors might lead you to feel attracted to someone. These factors can include body mass, height, and age—elements that play a significant role in many relationships.

However, other essential values that you should share are even more critical. There are six of them:

1. Children.
2. Religion.
3. Finances.
4. Personal or professional plans.
5. Family ties.
6. Resolve.

You might find it weird, but the happiness of many spouses has been challenged by the silence kept about this matter before marriage. The fear—we will talk about it in the next chapter—of losing that which seemed so precious at that moment—the love for someone so beautiful, so special, so fragile, so difficult to find—has restrained many from asking the right question and has brought them to catastrophic ends.

Values are fundamental to your future. If you have any uncertainty about their significance, talk about them to the person you're drawn to. Get answers and determine where you align or differ; this is essential. The groundbreaking should be done without challenges, through polite but direct questions. Hopefully, you will come to understand the values mentioned above better as you go over the pages of this book. And now we should talk about compatibility

Compatibility

There is a wrong notion about compatibility which defends the statement 'Marriage is not the place for fights.' Most people believe that if you fight, you are incompatible. This is far from the truth; every married couple will tell you that 'differences'—a term we might prefer over 'fights,' which suggests something more aggressive—are inevitable in any relationship.

Years ago, this friend of mine was about to marry his sweetheart against the opinion of several who had tried to discourage him. The problem was that they both 'fought' on petty and trivial things. Friends and family remarked that if they argued so much even before marriage, their future seemed bleak. As a friend, I thought differently but I did not express any opinion on the matter. They were free to do what they wanted most, and I did not have anything to say about it.

Among other things, they both knew very well what they were facing and had prepared for it wisely. The truth was that their differences were caused by the nervousness of a relationship that had lasted too long and the longing for each other in marriage. You must see them today: they are a loving couple, with many children and some grandchildren; their relationship matured through their generosity and the love that they have for each other.

Last 2022 in Barcelona, in a Congress organized by the International University of Cataluña under the title 'Family Accompaniment,' this Austrian psychologist specializing in 'trouble at home'—as he liked to put it—insisted on the fact that 'fights' are important and necessary. Most couples just need to figure out how to manage them. Fights are opportunities to start a dialogue in matters that, otherwise, would never have come out in the open and our psychologist recommends the therapy of agreement—which means, learning to iron out differences smoothly.

The point is that to understand compatibility we need to understand better human nature and for this, no better explanation has been given than the one found in the age-enduring, worldwide-bestseller known as the Bible. We read there that woman was taken from man. The Bible does not reason over the narrative[2] but its lesson seems to explain the intimate relationship between man and woman. The woman gained something from the man that no longer belongs to him; what the man lost can only be regained through her. Meanwhile, the man is the only one who can make the woman feel complete. Although both are fully independent, they need each other to be whole. Isn't it beautiful! Through marriage, man and woman become one again!

Masculinity and Femininity

But what is this that makes man and woman whole? Jokers often take things lightly and frequently overstep boundaries with remarks about their friends or people they encounter on the street. You could hear things like "How did that gorgeous woman end up with that ugly guy?" or "She may be broken, but hey, at least she snagged a rich husband!" or "He's a delight, but she's a drag," or "She's an accountant; the perfect match for a businessman," or "He's the quiet type, but no worries—she chatters away like a cockatoo." Do these comments reveal the deepest complementary insights in a relationship? Probably not.

Fig. 3. My Fair Lady.
(Courtesy of Warner Bros)

Have you ever heard of the movie *My Fair Lady*? Have you watched it? This musical comedy is quite delightful, though it might seem a bit dated for someone born at the turn of the twenty-first century.

Nonetheless, its themes are perfect for probing into our discussion on masculinity and femininity.

The movie, released in 1964 starring Audrey Hepburn and Rex Harrison, won eight Academy Awards and has been included in the list of the best one hundred movies of all time.[3] The story is quite simple. A renowned phonetics professor, Henry Hingis, embarks on the impossible experiment of turning an uneducated woman, Eliza Doolittle, into the likes of a duchess.

Professor Hingis is quite disappointed and because he blames her femininity for the lack of progress—something that he had always found difficult to understand—he sings: 'Why can't a woman be more like a man?'

Throughout the experiment, her femininity starts winning Henry over, but because of the ruthless treatment that she is receiving, she leaves him. Only then did Professor Hingis realize that he could not live without her.

The story is captivating, especially because it portrays each gender as distinct yet complementary.

Cormac Burke adds to the comment of Professor Hingis, 'Today he wouldn't be let get away with the remark without some people (not necessarily feminists) retorting: "and why can't a man be more like a woman?"... Young people are being educated to become de-sexed individuals, unisex citizens - not men and women. Frustration of true personal development is a main consequence of a unisex culture and education... The proper humanization of the person is severely limited, if one does not learn to distinguish and appreciate masculinity and femininity.'[4]

Unisex

The newly forged term, unisex, became popular during the so-called 'sexual revolution' of the sixties which glorified pleasure at any cost—above every existing rule and regardless of every damaging consequence. As we speak, we have not seen the end of it yet. New fashion companies seem determined to reshape contemporary culture by promoting unconventional, bizarre ways of dressing for men and women. They extreme a sexless fashion where men and women exchange the way they dress. Current trends defend that gender is not strictly binary and can be fluid, distinguishing it from biological sex. It is again the expression of Professor Hingis, "Why can't a woman be like a man?"—or the other way around, "Why can't a man be like a woman?"

Opinion does not equate to truth. Even if the popularity of these unprecedented ideas seems to be taking whole of the Western countries, a substantial majority of people understand that a man and a woman complement each other more naturally and straightforwardly in their expression of love. This is proven by the growth of the population all over the world—growth due to natural causes, not 'clones'—despite all slogans against it.

What the polls in the Western world show is tolerance for those who, despite being different from the majority, still have rights. It is interesting to see the power that a minority can exert over a majority. It is not surprising that the attempt to change the rules of the game has brought as a byproduct the decline in the number of children per family and the alarming number of separations and divorces. No wonder lovers today often find themselves haunted by fear and doubt!

We are facing one of the deepest crises of modern times in the understanding of what men and women are, but especially in the way they complement each other. We are risking the future of humanity.

'If we try to delineate these specifically feminine and masculine features, we find in women a unity of personality by the fact that heart, intellect, and temperament are much more interwoven, whereas in man there is a specific capacity to emancipate himself with his intellect from the affective sphere.'[5]

For a relationship to progress, it's essential to grasp how the man's and woman's innate traits contribute to their natural complementarity, highlighting his masculinity or her femininity. If the woman expects the man to be feminine and the man hopes for the masculinity of the woman, both will inevitably find themselves in a relentless struggle to fit within the family context.

'What matters in our context is to understand, first, that man and woman differ not merely in a biological and physiological direction, but that they are two different expressions of human nature; and second, that the existence of this duality of human nature possesses a great value.'[6]

Chapter Two: Harnessing Fear

It is normal to experience fear; it is a mistake to let fear control us. Every major step forward faces risk. Without risk there is no adventure and without adventure there is no thrill—and we might even lose meaning. Progress occurs only when we move forward; self-contained, stagnant attitudes lead to isolation. Sociologists demonstrate that isolated communities—whether physically or socially—are more likely to decline or disappear over time. Interaction, connection, and openness are essential for community vitality.

Without realizing it, today's culture causes us to build our lives on a paralyzing fear that turns us inwardly, driving us toward self-seeking behavior. Because of fear, we avoid situations that trigger anxiety or discomfort, we seek assurance from others, and we yearn for tranquility and pleasurable attitudes.

We might have inherited this disposition from the type of upbringing received at home rather than from a defect of character. This is not to say that we must blame our upbringing for it—because in the end everyone experiences fear—but know that our emotions are significantly shaped by our parents and siblings at home and continue to evolve as we journey through life.

You need not be rich to grow into a comfort-seeking type of upbringing. In one of the many off-road biking adventures through the beautiful landscapes of Cebu, we stopped for a while in a modest-looking, improvised café-hut to buy some soda (by the way, soda is recommended when you reach the point of exhaustion, a controversial issue between professional and amateur cyclists).

Fig. 4. You need not be rich to grow into a comfort-seeking type of upbringing.

A boy—around ten years old—sat on a bench next to our bikes and his mother came out three times to ask him what he wanted to have. The boy looked quite normal to me, but the mother came out with a Coke and with a straw and held it in her hands for the boy to suck the 'juice.'

Is the mother spoiling the kid? Maybe yes, maybe no; we don't know the circumstances. In a way, the Coke-and-straw anecdote seems to repeat itself in many modern homes today: children leading parents instead of the other way around.

Technology

Technology is leading us towards comfort-seeking ways too. How is that? Technology is spoiling us, making us lazy and self-centered.

Observe people in various settings, such as on public transportation, in restaurants, whether they are alone or in groups, and even in large gatherings. Their attention is wholly absorbed by their mobile phones, totally engrossed in their screens rather than in each other.

Today, you can find everything you need on your phone: news, music, movies, chat groups, games—which help detach oneself from a reality full of inconvenience and immerse us in a world of dreams—and much more.

If you are not careful, you might turn into FOMO—which stands for the 'Fear Of Missing Out'—a type of disorder that isolates the person even more. What ensues is an uncontrollable fixation on social recognition, which, via mobile phones, translates into emotional responses to the number of 'like' or reaction buttons that you collect, carrying the risk of depression when the social media crowd overlooks you.

Psychiatrists can tell you more, much more, about all this and how the brain functions are changing us—especially how the use of tablets and phones affects children. We do not know what we will become soon.

There are varying opinions regarding the advantages and disadvantages of electronics, but it is a fact that technology significantly influences decision-making, redefines life objectives, and alters behavior. This impact is particularly pronounced among younger generations who have not yet committed to a specific path.

The tragic fire at a certain call center—or remote management center—is a well-known incident. In the chaos of the forced evacuation, thirty agents noticed that their offices were still untouched by the flames and accessible. They asked the Incident Commander (IC) for permission to retrieve their personal electronic equipment. The IC allowed them to go up, but sadly, they never returned. This incident highlights the importance that the new generation place on their valuable gadgets. What would you do in a similar emergency?

Information technology is leading our lives today, facilitating the most banal needs, and making life easier. Gone are the days of strenuous work, prolonged training demands, and physical exertion—in a way, we all welcome progress. Priorities have changed; the focus is now on oneself. Companionship, which is a fundamental human need, has turned into a tool of convenience. Hence, any commitment is considered only in terms of the benefits it brings.

If we let comfortable standards lead our lives, if we don't fight these dispositions through a responsible and generous self-donation, we will always be controlled by the fear of losing the selfish comfort of what we enjoy—enlarged by the self-centered culture induced by technology. In a relationship, this fear will turn love into a calculator. The calculator indicates profit or loss and as we don't want to take a risk, we fall for further calculation and experimentation.

Premarital Sex

Because the pervasive environment is trying to bring about an idyllic new world based more on a movie script that in a real, down-to-earth, humanly acceptable reality, the rules of the game have changed for a vast number of people. The fear of a future together brings them to risk and experiment with premarital sex. They are not aware of the extreme physical and psychological impact of the trial that they are about to face, which can change their future for the worse.

You met someone whom you liked. You have been going out together for some time and your friendship has turned into an informal commitment; you believe you are in love. Then, suddenly, you—or your friend— say, 'Why don't we live together?'

This is a vintage issue. Timmy Thomas's[7] song "Why Can't We Live Together?" broadcasted this question back in the seventies. Later, Sade revisited the theme in her album *Diamond Life*, potentially offering a much-enhanced interpretation.

Fig. 5. Why would you turn your relationship into a living-in situation?

Tell me why, tell me why, tell me why
Mmm, why can't we live together?
Tell me why, tell me why
Mmm, why can't we live together?
Everybody wants to live together
Why can't we be together?

It is fashionable today—you might even say commonsensible, but you need to examine your feelings. Why would you turn your relationship into a living-in situation? Is this genuine love? Is love all about sex? Is it because you're curious about your friend's 5 am looks? Or are you secretly investigating his or her bathroom habits? You'll eventually uncover all the juicy details in the most unexpected, diverse ways.

Why then? Is it that you are balancing the benefits of a relationship, turning a living-in situation into an open excuse to experience sex?

Surely, you might have never thought about this but if sex is the only reason you commit to someone for life, you are going to be disappointed eventually and your relationship will just go down the drain. Over time, sexual appeal diminishes, and a person who considers it essential and abuses it may unknowingly be led toward pornography and infidelity.

Furthermore, if you engage in sex without a genuine, enduring, down-to-earth commitment to each other—which is essential to marriage—your disappointment may become so intense, even bordering on disgust, that you might lose interest in marriage altogether.

The same can be said for casual sex.

Disorder in a relationship can be compared to chaotic living conditions. Imagine a room where everything is out of place: books on the floor, clothes scattered everywhere, the bed unmade, plates with putrid leftovers, a dirty floor, and stains on the walls. Would you feel comfortable in this bedroom? After thrashing around for a while, you wouldn't want to stay there for long.

Fig. 6. Disorder in a relationship can be compared to chaotic living conditions.

Let's be honest and set things straight: when it comes to commitment, the heart is undeniably more essential than the sexual organ. And the heart calls for more than a temporary commitment; the heart wants it all: it is all or nothing. Permanency and exclusivity—don't pop stars sing the 'forever' song all the time? — are essential for a heart in love.

Permanency and Exclusivity

The turning point of every relationship, the step forward to commit to the unknown is overcoming the fear of permanency and exclusivity, the reason behind delays, uncertainties, doubts, insecurities, and the full gamut of emotions.

In the face of fear, how do we commit? What strategies can we use to overcome fear and make a commitment? True love harnesses fear. We learn to love sacrificing for one another to discover that happiness is in giving.

We must understand our heart and how it relates to love. We need to put aside whatever attempt to benefit from a sexual relationship leading us away from the genuine beauty of a commitment. We shall open our eyes and discover the needs of those around us instead of focusing on our selfish interests.

At this stage, we might still be wondering what is wrong with us because, despite any personal effort to overcome fear, we still notice a stubborn tendency to fall back and reconsider our choices. These feelings might be giving away other signs that were never thought of or considered seriously because not everyone is meant for married life.

Other expressions of self-donation are as important and necessary as marriage like the dedication to a spiritual commitment, the care of other family members, and a social or professional mission of service. These are all motivated by love and the conviction of being called to something special too. Love is the only thing that can give meaning to a life.

How are we going to prepare ourselves to become the giver and the recipient of love?

Maturity

Can we truly be selfless and put our heart and mind in another person? This is a puzzling question; somehow, disturbing. There is a lot we need to work on yet. For starters, we must mature in our love, because only love can bring a person to give oneself completely.

'There is no doubt that there are many people who have not known—or have not been able—to achieve the full development of their personality. Maturity necessarily leads to self-knowledge and knowledge of others. Knowledge that in turn leads to self-criticism and self-control.'[8]

While we might lack the extensive life experience that comes with decades of labor, a certain degree of maturity is essential to grasp the complexities of love. Maturity brings with it responsibility, regardless of age or status.

Although children typically depend on their parents or guardians for everything they do, some individuals retain childish attitudes throughout their lives.

To cultivate a sense of responsibility, conquer fears, and embrace a life of adventure, a combination of self-criticism, independence, and assurance is essential.

Maturity and responsibility harmonize seamlessly with a genuine zest for life.

Or, perhaps, it is that you haven't yet met the person you're meant to love. Deepening your understanding of love prepares you for when that special moment finally comes.

Chapter Three: Is It Love?

Your love is king[9] ... a beautiful, expressive phrase that touches the heart and tells a story: whether king or queen, love is special, exclusive, overpowering, and leaves no room for the plural form.

Fig. 7. Ask the old couples with a family that extends to children and grandchildren.

Love is so special that it changes the life of those who behold it. Because of love, people launch themselves into a beautiful life adventure, leave their past behind, and face an uncertain future, relying only on their commitment and determination. Love is more important than a bright future and the fullness of resources; it is the force behind it.

Ask the old couples with a family that extends to children and grandchildren: their life makes sense only around them. Their professional achievements are left behind as something unsubstantial. And most of them started on a meager salary and in a borrowed home.

Their determination, their willingness to overcome any obstacle along the way of marriage, and their fidelity and permanence speak of a true and generous love.

Forever Love

That deep desire for love is sung again and again by singers all over the world. Love songs have been a dominant theme in music across various genres and cultures for centuries.

"According to a study conducted in 2024, approximately 60% of all songs release in a given year are about love" (Repeat-Replay, 'What Percent of Song are about Love').

And what about "forever-love"? Many songs chase that dream, echoing words like "forever," "always," "eternity," and "never-ending."

True love, especially when we feel it in its most positive and emotional moments, tends to point toward permanence. And yet permanence is often what people fear most when entering a commitment.

Fear is expected; it is human. However, fear shouldn't be given the chance of dictating our actions.

Fig. 8. That deep desire for love is sung again and again by singers all over the world.

Fears often serve as warning signs, but we must identify their root causes. When fear stems from selfish attitudes or attachments, it becomes paralyzing. Fear of the unknown, however, is normal and can be managed. In a relationship, we moderate this fear by evaluating the core values that matter most—values highlighted throughout this book. Ultimately, courage is what enables us to move forward and commit: let the adventure begin.

Unfortunately, for many couples today, forming a family feels less like a dream and more like a threat to their ambitions. Beneath the pursuit of high-return careers, endless travel, and wealth often lies a fear—the fear of losing freedom, missing opportunities, or sacrificing personal success. In being so busy chasing these goals, many never come face-to-face with the "Angel of Love," perhaps without even recognizing it.

'The proportion of people getting married is going down in many countries across the world. Historical data from the United States shows that marriage rates have declined significantly since the early 20th century. Similar trends are observed in other rich countries. Non-rich countries also show a decline in marriages over the period 1990-2010.' [10] It is becoming clear over time that a serious development is underway, driven by a global shift in priorities.

Eventually, a meaningful, challenging professional life becomes a hustle after a few years and suddenly, people find themselves alone. It is already too late to find love. Their professional life has changed them into more self-centered, even selfish, persons. It is then more difficult to love because to see in a partner the 'king' or 'queen' of their youth, they must give themselves up and they are not willing to sacrifice what they have.

At this point, it is difficult to see virtue in the others and the person starts suffering from loneliness, sadness, and bitterness. Many mature individuals who have become isolated often trace their behavior back to missed chances of taking a stand for love in their younger years.

Loneliness

Loneliness is a seriously traumatic experience that places the person at risk. Studies on the matter reveal that 'Social isolation significantly increased a person's risk of premature death from all causes, a risk that may rival those of smoking, obesity, and physical inactivity. Social isolation was associated with about a 50% percent increased risk of dementia.'[11]

And it is not just happening among elderly people; studies reveal that the opposite is true: 'Loneliness is a common experience; as many as 80% of those under 18 years of age and 40% of adults over 65 years of age report being lonely at least sometimes, with levels of loneliness gradually diminishing through the middle adult years, and then increasing in old age (i.e., ≥70 years). Loneliness is synonymous with perceived social isolation, not with objective social isolation.'[12]

'The basic anthropological point is that the human person is not self-sufficient, but needs others... Each human person, in the awareness of his or her contingency, wishes to be loved: to be in some way unique for someone. Each one, if he or she does not find anyone to love him or her, is haunted by the temptation to feel worthless.'[13]

However, loneliness is not only caused by circumstances—such as "missing the chance." It is also a byproduct of isolation, often a self-made isolation carried under the banner of self-love and the popular expression "love your body."

Love Your Body is a song by French singer Amanda Lear released in 1983 by Ariola Records. Jennifer Lopez has been promoting body 'positivity' and self-love for many years, but her use of the expression 'Love Your Body' gained more prominence around 2015. She has often spoken about embracing her body and encouraging others to do the same, especially in the face of body-shaming and unrealistic beauty standards in Hollywood.[14]

'Love yourself' and 'Love your body' have altruistic components. However, the endless dissatisfaction of self-directed, self-contain desires and acts is an experience that we can all relate to. The end of it is a lonely life.

The feeling of selfish reciprocity is fleeting. The contrary, any act of selfless generosity for the sake of others, is truly meaningful. Genuine love and selflessness create a lasting impact, enriching both the giver and the receiver.

Self-love cannot keep up to the demand. Our ego cannot love back; we are just one, not two people.

Exclusive, true, and satisfying love is only possible between two. The desire for love is only satisfying outside oneself. This is part of our human nature. To fight it equates to going crazy.

If my goals revolve solely around myself, ignoring the broader purpose of living for others, achieving my objectives becomes meaningless, disappointing.

Fig. 9. Self-love cannot keep up to the demand. Our ego cannot love back.

If we don't fight selfish dispositions through a responsible and generous self-donation, we will always be controlled by the fear of losing the comfort of what we enjoy.

The remedy is within reach: let's put the needs of others ahead of our own. Let's cultivate a willingness to help and to sacrifice for others. And for those who believe that early marriage is incompatible with an active professional life, the fact that they can share family obligations with their spouse should put their worries to rest.

True love brings a couple to share responsibilities, making their life challenging, perfectly compatible with the strength of youth, something that a few years later is poised to become, if not cumbersome, exhaustive.

Manipulation

Few genuinely understand it; are you among them? The rest are heavily influenced by the negative environment created by the chaotic love lives of pop and movie stars, the unstable marriages of neighbors and relatives, and the organized population control campaigns targeting families. These factors are altering people's psyches. Can the unfortunate couple grasp the extent of the manipulation they face? Can they change their perspective? Is it possible to correct a misguided attitude?

The current generation's mindset idealizes marriage as the end goal—a finished, complete state where the couple finds solace, tranquility, and a paradise of happiness. Even with good advice, people often struggle to believe in the possibility of a happy married life when the essentials are missing. Some fail to understand that it's love that makes sacrifice and self-giving worthwhile in marriage. Ultimately, it all comes down to understanding the true essence of love.

Most people see love from the perspective of the recipient—which in a way we can now see as a somehow selfish attitude. Of course, you marry because the longing for each other is mutual but for starters, no foundation is stronger than each party's desire to love without conditions: love's first desire is the good of the other person.

Genuine Love

'Properly understood, and in the most immediate sense, love is only love to the extent that it concerns another person... Happiness is love's outcome, never its motive.'[15]

We genuinely love someone for what he or she is, not for the benefit that we draw from him or her; a true lover expects nothing in return.

Here we can understand the nature of the love for a sick person—suffering from a physical or mental illness or bent by age—who might be even indifferent to us or unable to express gratitude.

Just recently, I met the daughter of a good friend of mine—who unfortunately died some years ago—and had come back from abroad to lend a hand in the business of her family. Feeling like part of her family, we talked about her plans and her future. She then confided that she felt called to devote herself to the care of her impaired, physically ill sister. What a wonderful example of love! And what a wonderful legacy to my dear friend and his wife!

Love can manifest itself in many other ways like in the person that commits himself to a cause for God's sake or the welfare of a people.

Others sacrifice their careers to care for a family business and their parents or devote themselves to a demanding professional activity that will help many.

Fig. 10. We genuinely love someone for what he or she is, not for any personal benefit.

'Love's generous credit is intimately bound up with its surrender. The loving person in no way seeks his own gratification. He is oriented completely toward the other. And his trusting conviction is completely for the other's sake.'[16]

Is love measurable? Can we set limits? Can we rate self-giving? Do we have any tool that can help us to gauge love? It is important to understand that we all have deficiencies—and not just a few but out loud personality defects that might make life incredibly difficult for others.

The Love-Hurt Dichotomy

Defects are brought forward in every relationship. They are often translated into the common experience of hurt. Hurt is to love as a dog is to chase its tail. Hurt is experienced in a large variety of ways by everyone no matter what his or her views might be.

The love-hurt dichotomy, being as it is so common, can easily be treated. We need to give the right perspective to our feelings which, based on a growing love for the person we deal with, can be more easily controlled. It is easy to forgive when one acknowledges his or her defect and excuses the defects of the one he or she loves.

Feelings and emotions are triggered by mental states—respectively conscious and unconscious—that foster action or inhibit reaction.

'It is difficult to distinguish the difference between feelings and emotions... Emotions, especially those that are basic, are the automatic responses that appear before certain stimuli... Feelings are the subjective perceptions of emotions.'[17]

We can easily turn around our feelings when there is love; often the greatest obstacle is pride which can be sacrificed for the sake of love.

An emotional, impulsive surge of anger over a late arrival can be tempered by the feeling of understanding, reasoning the cause of the delay, or considering personality traits. We can always excuse behavior and turn our feelings around through affection. For this to happen, we need practice; instead of frowning, try to smile, say a kind word, or express your concern for the person—without irony. Once again, love and care can transform everything.

Unfortunately, many couples today turn their relationship into a battlefield over trivial matters that can be ironed out through affection. Remember that marriage will be your lifesaver—more important than any professional achievement or a 'bucket list'—which is safeguarded by mutual respect, a sincere concern for each other, time spent together, and eventually, physical contact.

Understanding the family dynamics broadly, working on the Family Project, turns every trial into a step up too, only comparable to the impetus given by the mission-vision statement of many public and private organizations and institutions.

Chapter Four: The Family Project

There is something mysterious, and personal about the word 'intimacy.' The Merriam-Webster dictionary describes it as 'something of a personal or private nature.' Other dictionaries define it in the context of a 'sexual relationship.'

While intimacy evokes a sense of closeness and deep connection among individuals—ranging from physical to emotional or intellectual—we prefer to consider it in the context of privacy or secrecy: intimacy is identity's most personal core value, intrinsically linked to dignity.

When we lose intimacy—when it is somehow made public—we lose dignity. Our identity, which is no longer personal, private, or secret, is put in danger. We expose ourselves to public scrutiny and the desires of those who have no right to intervene in our lives. Consequently, we lose the respect to which we are entitled.

Our identity is not just given by an ID or any other official document; it is more than that. Identity is given by our character and personality, by our ways and ideas, and by our gender—which is important to the point of defining what we are. Von Hildebrand ventures to say that 'In a certain sense, sex is the secret of the individual. Every disclosure of sex is the revelation of something intimate and personal.' It is bad taste to talk about personal issues related to sex in public, even among friends.

Fig. 11. This is the marvelous thing about spousal love.

If sex is so intimate, personal, and so deeply related to one's identity, what can explain spousal love? Regardless of what the definitions of intimacy say, isn't it that when a person openly discloses oneself to another, he or she violates the extremely basic principle of intimacy? Isn't it a betrayal of the person's identity?

This is the marvelous thing about spousal love which gives complete meaning to the sexual life of every person: the spouses, through the marriage commitment and the gift of each other, have become just one. Their bodies have fused into one.

The marital relationship has turned into an overwhelming, joyful act, driving the couple into a unique and different world of love, happiness, tenderness, and contentment that cannot be experienced in any other way. Only within the respect, secrecy, and privacy of the marital relationship, do the couples' empowering bloom.

When sex is reduced to mere pleasure-seeking—often expressed as "Let's have sex"—and lacks the deeper dimensions of intimacy (secrecy), respect (loving care), exclusivity (fidelity), permanency (through sacrifice), self-giving (mutual generosity), and fruitfulness (openness to a meaningful creation), its appeal gradually diminishes. Eventually, this erosion of significance leads to the couple's decision to separate because they can no longer tolerate each other.

This is what today's young people are exposed to by an uncontrollable propaganda that hates humanity and everything that represents it—this is tough saying but, how can you explain this prejudice? It is difficult to understand the logic behind these self-destructive and suicidal tendencies—the species' self-annihilation that seems to echo the growing number of people taking their own lives in many countries. We can only ask ourselves: what's going on?

It is easy to follow fashionable attitudes; what is difficult is to rebel against them, be daring, and challenge a world that dictates to every aspect of our lives and every thought we nurture.

A happy marriage is built on true love, a selfless love that desires, first, the good for the other person. The test of love is cherishing the fruits of that union. 'Are you referring to children?' What else? Pets? A booming business? This might be shocking for some but yes, we are talking about children.

On a transoceanic flight from Europe, Michael—Mickey among his friends—sat across the aisle from a young mother with her one-year-old baby.

The baby—following a longstanding tradition believed to have started at the beginning of humanity, humor me—was crying and crying.

A gentleman of about fifty years of age sat near the mother and her child and kept on complaining.

The environment in the flying compartment was tense. This was a long flight, and the complainant was not willing to shut up—which perhaps encouraged the child to shriek even more.

Then, the not-so-gentle man stood up and faced the mother.

At that point, Mickey who had sympathized with the mother from the very beginning, saw the child, propelled by the mother, land across the aisle on his lap, and the mother attacked the man with such fury that the passengers had a tough time separating them.

Shall I Marry? — 43

Fig. 12. The not-so-gentle man stood up and faced the mother.

When order was restored, the man asked the flight steward for a different seat, but she instead addressed the woman with the child and invited her to sit in first-class accommodations. The whole cabin burst into a long and loud applause.

We will not judge the attitude of the not-so-gentle man. We can only wonder, what type of person dislikes children? What can we say about him or her? If children don't have a place in his or her heart, what can you find there? Bringing the anecdote to the level of our discussion, who could wish to marry and dislike children at the same time? What type of heart does a spouse who does not want children in the family have?

Legacy

The sincerity of that longing for each other in marriage is manifested in the couple's desire for a legacy, in the children—which, within nature, not everyone might be able to enjoy it. The family is the only natural environment where a child can find the same love that brought him or her about. Pets instead of kids—pets are good but not as a substitute—denaturalize and endanger the union husband-wife, showing that marriage was only calculated. The couple will eventually realize that their union does not make sense and will end up separating.

You will notice in published statistics that temporary commitments are not usually fruitful. Data from the US tells us that 66% of divorced couples are childless.[18]

Statistics show you the level of manipulation we are subject to: people don't want children, but they still want a legacy because 'people are people.' Did you notice that men and women have an overwhelming desire for perpetuation? Years ago, the saying went: 'Have a child, write a book, and plant a tree.' Now the word 'child' has been removed from the equation, but the desire for perpetuation remains. Few manage the honor of naming a street through professional achievements but most of us can still leave graffiti on a stone or a tree—now punishable by law—on a mountain trail or worse, on any wall along the way.

'Man does understand that his life alone does not endure and that he must therefore strive to exist in others, to remain through them and in them in the land of the living.'[19] The true legacy of love is in the children. Children might feel like a challenge before marriage but eventually, they turn out to be the secret of love and fidelity, the perpetuation of the union, and the meaning to their lives.

Your legacy, your children, are part of your Family Project, the project of a lifetime, born of a longing for love, managed by sacrifice and the desire to make your family the center of your life—and even if you could, transforming it into the paradise so much waited for. Your Family Project will not only change your life but also the life of everyone around you: you will influence society and, eventually, contribute to a better world.

'As they await their wedding day, an engaged couple work happily on so many projects - minor and even trivial projects, in themselves - that will help to make up their new life together... Is it possible, then, for them not to thrill together with enthusiasm at the major project that nature has reserved for them, a project that will be uniquely theirs and exclusive to their union; ... a genuine creation on their part (with God's collaboration) of living beings, their own children...?'[20]

Investing in Your Future

Let me tell you about my friend Robert and a conversation with his seatmate on a chance flight from a business trip to China. On his way back to Davao, this Chinese businessperson insisted on sharing his research on family investments—he seemed overly excited about his discovery. He had studied the returns of several life insurance policies against the average family population—or number of children per family. His conclusions would shock any population-control activist: for an ordinary man and woman to harvest the returns of a lifetime investment in the family, the couple should have no less than five children!

He never explained to Robert what the base population of his study was and how he had collected the data, but he recommended investing in children instead of insurance policies because the returns were higher and safer. When you grow old, your children take care of you—assuring that you have taken care of them—and having five children avoids the burden that you and your wife might place on a single child—even on two—which seems to be most fashionable today. No insurance company will visit you, bring you to the hospital when you need it, help you with your most banal needs, pay your bills—and collect your pension, and give you love and grandchildren to lift your spirit and turn the last days of your life into a retirement bliss.

Not everyone is given the chance to have a large family. Some face challenges and even crises that recommend evaluation. Whatever the reasons for limiting the number of children, think very seriously about the projection of a decision that can affect the future and even the harmony within the family: would you be placing at risk the evidence of your love, your love without conditions? Won't you be giving up on your Family Project, showing how poor your convictions are? Aren't you doubting everything you promise to your spouse?

We certainly doubt; we certainly give up often on what we started and easily turn from jaguars to kittens. You need a dependable, faithful, moral, and spiritual adviser who can help you both—often separately: you need help.

Natural Family Planning

A trusted adviser can help you analyze the circumstances that recommend postponing the arrival of children. But to preserve the honesty of your feelings, you need to follow nature and reject the obvious misguided propaganda about the use of artificial methods of contraception. Artificial methods violate the reverence that a couple should show to their life-giving power, the truthfulness of spousal love—and even the satisfaction that it brings with it, treating something so lovable as a sickness. Violence is evident when artificial interventions disrupt nature's course. In a way, it is cheating nature, and eventually, the consequences of deceit catch up with the deceiver.

Dietrich von Hildebrand comes once again to help us in this matter. He explains that 'The intention to avoid conception does not imply irreverence as long as one does not actively interfere in order to frustrate it [through artificial means of contraception]. Nor is the use of natural family planning in order to avoid conception in any way irreverent, because the very fact of the possibility of natural family planning, that is to say, the fact that conception is limited to a short period, includes also a God-given institution.'[21]

The woman's natural cycles indicate that family planning is possible within nature.[22]

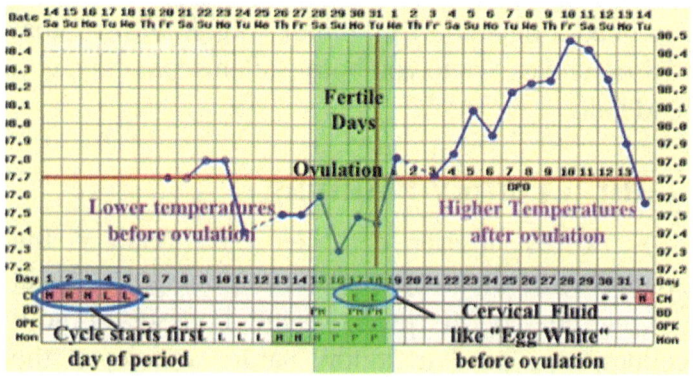

Fig. 13. Natural Family Planning. The Symptothermal Method (www.fertilityfriend.com).

The decision to postpone the arrival of children in a family is usually triggered by financial considerations; the future of the family is limited by the financial stability of the spouses. This is a main issue that might bring up doubts even about the advisability of marrying: it is obvious that together with love the couple needs 'money.' Here again, extreme, obsessive, and pervasive attitudes are dangerous too—like waiting to complete any dream before the actual marriage happens or putting money first on the scale of priorities.

Relax. Make sure that you plan for what is necessary and let the feeling of adventure take over. Some might disagree on this matter but, if there is no adventure, there is no thrill, and if there is no thrill, there is no way you can look forward to the dream of a lifetime. The Family Project—like taking up studies, learning a skill, starting in a new company, formulating a strategy, working on a new venture, ...—is just a work in progress: you do not know what will come out of it.

As your family's finances depend so much on your earnings, you must find ways of performing better without compromising family obligations. Fast money is a fallacy. You need to prove your value through skills—which must grow—and honesty; through permanence and openness to those who trusted you—gaining the sympathy of your superiors and keeping them informed of your plans before moving on to another company.

If you need to work abroad, try to bring the family with you—even if it means limiting your income; if you need to work multiple jobs, make sure to keep active and regular contact with your family.

Character development, training on best family practices, and spiritual support should complement your Family Project: we all need to grow; we all need to change for the better. As an added benefit, we also count on the fellowship of many other families that we can contact through international associations, [23] families who share the same values and understand the importance of working on their own Family Projects without discouragement.

Difficulties along the way are not obstacles to a family that has the support of a spiritual foundation. We are more than just another biological species on the planet: we are the only ones who are conscious of a purpose and a mission; the only ones who realize that if we do our best, we will always count on the help of God.

Chapter Five: I Got Some Questions

The following paragraphs thematically separated, are like a summary of your readings. Within the context of our conversation, you'll discover questions designed to aid your reflection. Bring up the discussion to your sweetheart or even better, let him or her read the book and comment on it. The core values brought up and expanded are taken from Chapter 1, 'I Like You.' This section offers deeper insights into their meanings and presents scenarios to support your problem-solving efforts. While slightly more extensive than the preceding chapters, these ideas underscore the guide's crucial importance for your future.

Values

What outstanding values attracted you to the person you are dating? When it comes to considering the possibility of starting a family, the most attractive qualities in your soulmate often extend beyond physical appearance. While initial attraction might be sparked by physical chemistry, deeper values, and character traits are what truly matter. Can you identify the most significant value that led you to consider starting a family one day?

Are you primarily attracted to your sweetheart for his or her sexual appeal, or do character and personality play a more significant role? A durable foundation is built on emotional connection, shared values, and mutual respect. Focusing solely on sexuality can lead to hollow relationships.

Have you ever struggled with an attachment to pornography? If so, have you sought guidance from a spiritual adviser or a doctor? Open communication with the right person and self-reflection are essential in understanding and addressing any potential issues.

What is your attitude toward your soulmate? Is it caring? How often do you use your mobile phone when you are together? Do you ask permission to use it? Body language plays a significant role in relationships. When spending time with your loved one, being present and attentive is crucial. Excessive use of mobile phones during face-to-face interactions can send negative signals. Remember, these seemingly trivial details can convey deeper dispositions.

Do you have heated discussions? Do you clash with each other about almost every issue you bring up in a conversation? Or do you simply disagree with the alternative solution? Reflect on the cause behind differences and the values that you share.

Fig. 14. How often do you use your phone when you are together?

Try to agree on the basics and be open to opinions and options. Work on the personality traits that make you aggressive or intolerant. You might need a radical change of attitude or to find out what helps you most to remain calm and in control. Smile often and hold hands when you feel the wrong emotions rising in your heart.

How respectful are you towards your soulmate? In a relationship, just as chivalry is appreciated in men, kindness and empathy are often highly valued in women. These qualities create a nurturing and supportive environment, fostering emotional connection and understanding.

Feelings

Can you put into words your feelings toward your sweetheart? Let me laugh at this now because very often people find it difficult to express their feelings and you, most probably, are not the exception. But try it. What would you say to express your affection? But please, do not use the worn-out expression, 'I love you.' Be more creative.

Does the word 'longing' fit as a stand-up feeling? If it doesn't, reflect on what you understand of love and try to compare it to the idea of giving yourself for the sake of love, not for your benefit and convenience. What would you do for your sweetheart? This feeling should be mutual, not just one-sided.

It's essential to consider whether you see your soulmate as your complementary half. Do you appreciate his or her qualities as a man or woman? Understanding masculinity and femininity can enrich your relationship. If you haven't explored the topic, consider reading materials that shed light on these aspects.

Let me ask you another personal question, only for your musing, something that is better discussed with your spiritual adviser: are you serious about your marriage? Do you have the disposition to remain beside your spouse for years, no matter what happens? In other words, are you willing to sacrifice yourself for the permanence and exclusivity of your marriage, for the love of your spouse?

Children

Discussing children is crucial. Are you afraid to broach this topic with your fiancé/fiancée? If you've already talked about it, reflect on his or her response. If your soulmate doesn't want children, it's a key issue for your future; perhaps you could recommend dialoguing about this matter with a person who could help his or her understanding. You are free to do whatever you think is right; just study how to turn this crucial concern around and give it some time before you decide.

Professional Plans

Would your professional ambitions get in the way of your marriage? A professional career is perfectly compatible with a married man or a married woman. If you add financial considerations—your basic needs, the professional career becomes your highway.

Still, remember that all highways have traffic signs limiting your speed, telling you to turn right or left when needed, warning you of slippery surfaces, and pointing the direction you must follow to get to your destination. Marriage is like that. You need to see your professional career within the loving needs of your family.

You might have to sacrifice personal ambitions for the family. We have all heard of people who, because of the need of their immediate or extended family, change jobs or give up professional status and ability. At times, the need to sacrifice personal, honest ambitions comes in unexpected ways like when considering an earlier marriage rather than a postponement.

The best time to start a family is when both man and woman are in the prime or the physical and mental capacity to start an adventure. This is when everything seems easier, and the feeling of love is stronger. But don't get it wrong: there should be a foundation; there should be something that we could call the infrastructure of the Family Project. The structural plans are always drawn ahead, and the building pillars are always first, the starting point of what is to come up, the planning that everyone should do before starting a family. Unfortunately, today, many are only satisfied by full-scale, completely developed state ventures. Often a house is not enough; you need a golf course beside it. Reason about this: if you have it all, you will just feel enraged to lose it or miss it. Lower your expectations and dare to feel the challenge!

Religious Affiliation

Let's discuss another crucial matter, often considered private—a senseless taboo in many Western countries: religious affiliation. Have you talked to your fiancé/fiancée about his or her religious feelings and the depth of his or her religious commitment? Like our previous discussion about children, religious affiliation is significant and must be openly discussed and respected. Each spouse should feel trust, confidence, love, and the freedom to follow his or her conscience on religious convictions. Respect plays a vital role.

While it's ideal to marry within the same religious denomination or belief, the cosmopolitan world we live in today often brings together people from diverse backgrounds. Still, it's essential to reach an agreement about the education of your children. Understanding each other's beliefs and finding common ground ensures a harmonious family life.

Unpredictably, a person might feel upset if the future spouse chooses to raise the children in a different religious denomination than his or her own. Again, agreements should follow but, if disagreement persists, a time for reflection is needed before committing to marriage and the aid of a spiritual adviser is highly recommended.

Relatives

Are you on good terms with your in-laws? What type of problems have you encountered? What about family ties? As a way of speaking, we refer to family ties in the context of the influence that the immediate family might exert on issues of your concern only. We are not talking about likes and dislikes from parents or future in-laws, so common everywhere, but about the relatives' pressure to influence the core values under discussion.

I know of marrying couples with different religious backgrounds which were not accepted by the extended family because of their convictions and their ideas regarding the children's upbringing. Would this become a problem for you? Is this something about which you should worry? Others have radically opposed marriage because, even when having the same cultural background, they were of different races. Often in these two cases—religious and racial differences—the pressure is likely to break your ties with the family. This situation can turn into a nightmare if you are working for a family corporation and your professional future is at stake.

It is important to keep the emotions under control and find ways of discussing understanding. Often, this situation is temporary. Feelings change after a time when you prove and show your love for your spouse that extends to your in-laws too, despite differences.

You might have been worrying about the influence of relatives over your future spouse too. You wonder whom you are marrying, your fiancé/fiancée or your mother-in-law/father-in-law? Is that tolerable? Would it be appropriate? Would you talk to your fiancé/fiancée and try to make sense out of it? This is a pressing issue that should not be left for later. Even when the opinion of your relatives or your in-laws is always welcome, the ultimate decision is taken between you and your spouse, avoiding interference.

Fig. 15. Your extended family is a pressing issue that should not be left for late.

The financial status of your in-laws, problems related to their employment, and even cultural traits—like relatives moving into your new home—might pose a problem if you are supposed to help them.

Will you earn enough to support not only yourself and your spouse but also your extended family? Is there any sensible way you can dissuade them or at least avoid the added responsibility?

Given meticulous consideration, it is not easy to make a decision that might impact the relationship. It is also important to work on each situation patiently and through dialogue to keep family ties open and friendly. Family ties are as important as professional deals; for centuries, both were equated. If in the Western world, family ties appear inconsequential, this is not the case in continents like Asia and Africa, where the family forms the strongest, most basic structure—the very strands of textile fibers weaving the fabric of society.

You are naturally free to act most appropriately when dealing with a significant concern. However, you would probably appreciate the advice of a competent third party—still, assuming full responsibility for your action—without blaming others for the consequences.

"Am I too old to get married?"

"Am I too old to get married?" Some individuals may have never received the necessary support to understand the true essence of his or her call to marriage. Others were deeply engrossed in professional, family, social, and moral obligations, which recommended postponing marriage.

Fig. 16. "Am I too old to get married?"

Now, they find themselves facing this dilemma. But fear not; it is never too late. Within these pages, you'll discover everything you need to take those first steps toward commitment. Let the feeling of adventure sweep over you; suddenly, you'll feel young again, re-energized.

However, don't sacrifice your core values for the sake of a shared future. When a relationship remains childless, it's essential to explore alternative ways to express love to each other and the community. Always show extra care for your spouse, but also find a personal project to devote yourself to. Find out if you can help other families; extend your care to those in need; and perhaps, embrace the role of nurturing children beyond your own. In doing so, you'll find purpose and fulfillment, regardless of age.

Remember, when there is love, it's never too late to embark on this beautiful journey.

Hurt

Lastly, let's talk about the hurt and the emotional drive. Would you bet on the chances of you changing your wrong ways? Very often people think of themselves as excusable and entitled to special treatment: all of us think much on terms of rights but little on duties. Experiencing hurt is not wrong; surprisingly, it makes us feel real, human, and spiritual. It also gives us a feeling of hope, the hope of finding what we want, and, eventually, the hope of changing for the love of a commitment. If we love, we will wish to change for the better.

How is this translated into your day-to-day life? We all need to be positive about our relationship with those we love because hope and optimism are the forces we need to overcome hurt. We love, first, because we see our deficiencies and then understand the deficiencies of others. Even more, his or her deficiencies might even make us laugh because he or she is that way and we love it, even if we would welcome his or her chances of changing.

Let me tell you about these nameless friends of mine. An unavoidable commitment in another city required the wife to be absent herself during the couple's wedding anniversary. Her friends in the distant city decided to surprise her with a bouquet of flowers, supposedly from her husband. She was very appreciative but as soon as the group separated, she approached the leader and asked her: 'How much was it? I will pay you back.' She added, 'For you to know that my husband, never, ever, has given me a bouquet of flowers on any anniversary!' They ended up laughing merrily and celebrating his ways. She loved her husband to the point of distraction!

Conclusion

All along these pages, issues related to current misunderstandings and outright crises in families have been outlined, making our modern times perhaps one of the more challenging periods in the history of humanity because the family is at the base of the pyramidal structure of society. And without the family, without the right foundation for the family, it is not possible to build a human world.

The values brought up and sketched in this short book are like the A to Z for anyone who feels the need to set things right from the very beginning of his or her new adventure. Still, let me underline the fact that not everyone is called to marry. Each one needs to find his or her way, his or her calling, but a calling of love.

Allow me to conclude this chapter by telling you again about Lance, the protagonist from the *Introduction*. Fate led me to casually meet him sometime later in my new country; we had never met before. Lance and I became good friends, and over time, he confided in me, sharing his life story. To my surprise, I discovered that the abandoned fiancée was the sister of someone I knew!

Lance's path diverged from the conventional. He never married, and as the years passed, he quietly left this world. His departure was felt deeply by those of us who cherished his friendship. Yet, there was comfort in knowing that he left in peace with God. His was an uncommon story with a beautiful ending—one that we all hope for in our journeys.

Sometimes, the most unexpected connections and stories weave together to create a touching tapestry of life.

A well-known, often-cited Spanish poet by the name of Antonio Machado immortalized these feelings in the words, *Let each traveler follow his own path*. Whatever path we follow, let it be fruitful, let's leave a trail of good, let this be done through love and faithfulness.

Tex

Acknowledgments

Let each traveler follow his own path. Though single, I could say that I have married and remained faithful to the dozens and dozens of friends whom I have advised over the years in matters related to personal growth, preparation for marriage, and the enrichment of their family life. I have always seen in their eyes their appreciation and thankfulness. The topics highlighted in this short book are a part of that effort.

Seeking support, I shared the final draft with my friends. Despite their busy schedule—juggling intense professional work and caring for their large families—they all expressed keen interest in reviewing the manuscript. As a Volunteer of Educhild Foundation Inc., I extend my heartfelt gratitude to Noemi and Diosdado (DM) Marasigan, our President, for their unwavering encouragement.

Linda and Ed Fadullon found the book useful for discussions with their adult children, and their daughter Isa enjoyed the trendy topics. Carol and Noli Pineda carefully reviewed the manuscript and found it highly relevant. Reggie and Raffy Mendoza provided very encouraging feedback.

I am also indebted to those who unknowingly bolstered my tenacity during the writing process.

Among them, I'd like to thank Elaine and Boyet Quinto, Cyndia and Agustin Morales, Alexandra and Niko Escobal, Kim Ranosa, Jo Montales, and the countless, impossible list of friends within the Educhild family across the Philippines, whose collective support has been invaluable.

Acknowledgments are a beautiful way to express gratitude to those who contributed to your journey. I would like to think of the Educhild family on those terms and make use of the occasion to tell their contribution to the uplifting of family values in the Philippines since the informal gathering of the first volunteers on the 14th of February of 1976.

The words of DM in the 'Foreword' page of the recently published work *The Educhild Story*, [24] summarize the importance of what has been transcribed, that the 'Family is the bedrock of our lives. It is the place we return to for love, understanding, commitment, and a sense of belonging.'

About the Author

The author–by the nickname of Tex, obtained a Licentiate in Biology with a specialization in Zoology from the State University of Valencia, Spain. He also completed a Certificate in Education at the University of Alicante, which qualified him for teaching positions. Additionally, he holds a Diploma in Affectivity and Sexuality from the University of Navarre in Spain.

In the Philippines he ventured into other fields to add to his humanistic and technical formation finishing a master's in library and information sciences by the University of the Philippines in Diliman, that he completed with a sub specialty in library software and history and the publication of articles in specialized journals together with the printing of the book *History of Books and Libraries in the Philippines, 1521-1900*. He has also published software for library management.

He has occupied management positions in cultural centers, lectured extensively about value education, engaged in school consultancies, mentoring, and counseling. He is an avid cyclist and motorist and has been everywhere North to South in the Philippines.

Other Works by the Author

Tex Hernandez is the author of several thought-provoking books that explore some of life's biggest questions—touching on values like personal growth, relationships, identity, and decision-making. His works are brought together under the engaging umbrella of *The Big-Question Series*, with each title offering a fresh take on challenges we all face.

Am I an Atheist? Science, Atheism, and the Way of Friendship – A thoughtful look at the relationship between science and belief, and how both shape the way we connect with others.

Should I Marry? The Essential Guide to Discernment – A guide to understanding what makes commitment meaningful and how it relates to happiness and lasting success.

Shall I Dress It? Sexuality in Overdrive – An eye-opening examination of the powerful pull of sexuality, including perspectives on addiction and identity.

What Are My Chances? Life Management Explained – A practical and inspiring guide to navigating life's choices and finding a sense of purpose through planning.

Why Character? The Quest That Matters – The newest addition, offering fresh insights into character development through five essential pillars.

All titles in *The Big-Question Series* are available online via Google Play Books and Amazon Kindle Store.

NOTES

1 Song Seung-hyun, 'Unspoken code of K-cool,' *Asia News Network (ANN)*, in *The Korea Herald*, June 4, 2024 (asianews.network/unspoken-code-of-k-cool).

2 In Genesis 2, verses 21 to 22 it is said: "So the Lord God caused a deep sleep to fall upon the man, and while he slept took one of his ribs and closed up its place with flesh; and the rib which the Lord God had taken from the man he made into a woman and brought her to the man."

3 Wikipedia, "My Fair Lady (film)," June 20, 2024 (wikipedia.org).

4 Cormac Burke, Covenanted Happiness (Third Edition, 2011), 'Sexuality and Sexual Identity,' pp. 10-12.

5 Dietrich von Hildebrand, *Man and Woman* (Manchester, New Hampshire: Sophia Institute Press, 1992), 'Men and women differ essentially,' p. 29.

6 *Ibid.*, p. 30.

7 *Timmy Thomas, whose spellbinding anti-war song 'Why Can't We Live Together' was a global hit in 1973... With its organ chords, rudimentary drum machine rhythm and heartfelt vocals from Thomas, 'Why Can't We Live Together' remains one of the most striking and minimalist R&B songs of the 1970s. It reached No 3 in the US and No 12 in the UK; its lyrics of pacifism and racial harmony chimed with listeners amid the still-raging Vietnam war.* "Timmy Thomas, R&B singer," The Guardian, 14 March 2022 (theguardian.com).

8 Martí García, Miguel-Ángel, *La Madurez, Dar a las cosas la importancia que tienen* (Madrid: Ediciones Internacionales Universitarias, 2004; Quinta Edición), p. 13.

9 'Your Love Is King' is a song by English band Sade from their debut studio album, Diamond Life (1984). The song was written by Sade Adu and Stuart Matthewman, and produced by Robin Millar. It was the album's lead single in the UK, released in January 1984, and the third single in the US. The album eventually went on to achieve an astonishing 4x platinum certification in both the UK and US, selling more than seven million copies worldwide. 'Your Love in King,' 'Diamond Life,' 15 July 2024 (em.m.wikipedia.org).

10 Copilot, response to "The most reliable worldwide statistics on Marriage," OpenAI, June 20, 2024. The data is sourced from multiple reliable sources, including statistical country offices, UN reports, Eurostat, and the OECD. In summary, the Our World in Data platform is a valuable resource for understanding global marriage trends and patterns. You can find more detailed information on their website (ourworldindata.org). The World Marriage Data 2019 provides comparable information on the marital status of the population by age and sex for 232 countries (population.un.org).

11 CDC, 'Loneliness and Social Isolation Linked to Serious Health Conditions,' *Alzheimer's Disease and Health Aging*, April 29, 2021 (cdc.gov/aging/publications/features/lonely-older-adults.html).

12 Louise C. Hawkley and John T. Cacioppo, 'Loneliness Matters: A Theoretical and Empirical Review of Consequences and Mechanisms,' *PubMed Central*, in *NIH The National Library of Medicine*, December 30, 2013 (ncbi.nlm.nih.gov/pmc/articles/PMC3874845/).

13 Burke, *Covenanted Happiness*, 'What marriage is for,' p. 55.

14 Marie Claire, '8 Quotes That Prove Jennifer Lopez Is The Queen Of Body Confidence,' 2015 (https://www.marieclaire.co.uk/news/beauty-news/jennifer-lopez-body-quotes-118759?form=MG0AV3).

15 Von Hildebrand, *Man and Woman*, 'The Nature of Love,' pp. 8 & 10.

16 *Ibid.*, 'Love Surrenders,' pp. 24-25.

17 Laura Alonso Gonzalez, 'Do you know the difference between feelings and emotions?' *Ifeel*, December 3, 2021 (ifeelonline.com/en/online-therapy/do-you-know-the-difference-between-feelings-and-emotions).

18 The Law Office of Molly B. Kenny, 'By the Numbers: Childless Couples are more likely to divorce,' October 23, 2023 (mollybkenny.com/blog); Andrea Whatcott, 'Childless couples still divorce at a much higher rate than those with children,' August 3, 2011 (deseret.com).

19 Joseph Ratzinger, *Introduction to Christianity* (Ignatius Press: San Francisco, 2004), p. 262.

20 Burke, *Covenanted Happiness*, 'What has gone wrong with marriage today?' p. 73.

21 Von Hildebrand, *Man and Woman*, 'How contraception differs from natural family planning,' pp. 55-56.

22 The Symptothermal Method (STM) is a highly effective Fertility Awareness-Based Method (FABM), combining basal body temperature (BBT) tracking with cervical mucus monitoring (and sometimes calendar tracking) to pinpoint ovulation, allowing couples to either avoid or plan pregnancy by identifying fertile days, with no side effects but requiring diligent daily charting. By observing a slight rise in temperature after ovulation and changes in mucus (becoming clear, stretchy like egg whites), users can determine their fertile window and abstain from intercourse during that time to prevent pregnancy, or time intercourse to conceive.

23 Let me tell you about the International Federation for Family Development (IFFD), a non-governmental, independent, and non-profit federation, whose primary

mission is to support families through training. Counting on a General Consultative Status with the UN Economic and Social Council (ECOSOC), the IFFD programs work in 68 countries across 5 continents in collaboration with an extensive network of volunteers. You can contact them through their website and ask about their programs in your country (iffd.org).

24 Mina, Achilles, Editor in Chief, *The Educhild Story, From Playgrounds to Promising Futures* (Manila: Media Wise Communications, Inc./ Muse Books, 2023).

Made in the USA
Coppell, TX
28 February 2026

72589623R00049